DOES THE MOON CHANGE SHAPE?

*Thanks to Thomas Affatigato, Children's Program Director of
the Vanderbilt Planetarium for his helpful comments on the
concepts presented in this book*

Cover illustration: ERNEST S. ALBANESE

Library of Congress number: 89-3647

Library of Congress Cataloging in Publication Data

Goldish, Meish.
   Does the moon change shape? / Meish Goldish; illustrated by Susan Dodge.

   (Real readers)
   Summary: An explanation of the phases of the moon for beginning readers.
   1. Moon—Phases—Juvenile literature. [1. Moon—Phases.] I. Dodge, Susan, ill.
II. Title. III. Series.
QB588.G64 1989   523.3′2—dc19   89-3647
ISBN: 0-8172-3518-3

1 2 3 4 5 6 7 8 9 0   93 92 91 90 89

REAL READERS

Does the Moon Change Shape?

by Meish Goldish

illustrated by Susan Dodge

Raintree Publishers
Milwaukee

You can see the **moon** at night. You see the moon up in the sky.

Some nights the moon looks big. It looks like a big **O**.

On other nights the moon does not look so big. It looks like a fat **D**.

Some nights the moon looks like a **C**. You can see just a little bit of it. And on some nights you can't see the moon at all.

Does the moon really change shape?

The moon does <u>not</u> change shape. It's always shaped like a big ball. It just looks like it is changing shape.

The moon does not have light of its own. You see the moon because of light that comes from the **sun**.

The sun shines on the **earth**, where you are. It shines on the moon, too.

You and a friend can show how the sun's light shines on the moon. You will need a dark room, a flashlight, and a ball.

Pretend the flashlight is the sun. Pretend you are the earth and that the ball is the moon.

Your friend will stand still and hold the flashlight, so that it does not move. You begin by standing with your back to your friend. Your friend will shine the flashlight up over your head. You hold the ball up so that you can see one **whole** side of it.

The ball looks like a big **O** in the light.

Your friend keeps standing still. But now you turn in place to the left. Turn till your left side is facing your friend.

The light still shines on the ball. But you and the ball have moved. So you can see less of the ball.

The part you can see looks like this:

Turn left again. Turn till you are facing your friend. Now the light shines on the side of the ball you can't see.

You can hardly see the ball at all.

Keep turning left till your right side is facing your friend. The part of the ball you can see looks like this: ◐

Now keep turning left till you are standing with your back to your friend. You are back to where you began. Again the part of the ball you can see looks like a big **O** in the light.

Is the ball changing shape? No. What changes as you turn is how much of the ball you can see in the light.

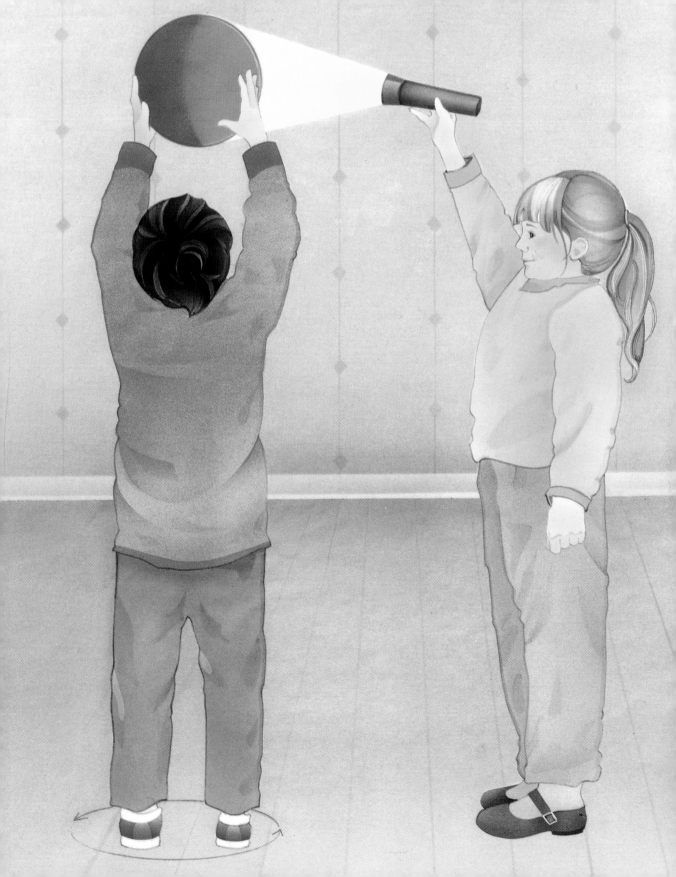

You and your friend just showed how the moon moves around the earth. It takes about 30 days, or one **month**, for this to really take place.

The sun is always shining, like the flashlight. The earth and the moon keep turning, like you and the ball. The moon's shape seems to change because of how much of the moon you can see in the sun's light.

Sunday	Monday	Tuesday	Wednesday	Thursday	Friday	Saturday
					1	2
3	4	5	6	7	8	9
10	11	12	13	14	15	16
17	18	19	20	21	22	23
24	25	26	27	28	29	30

For a small part of the time each month, you can see a moon that looks like this:

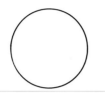

This is called a **full moon**.

Sunday	Monday	Tuesday	Wednesday	Thursday	Friday	Saturday
					1	2
3	4	5	6	7	8	9
10	11	12	13	14	15	16
17	18	19	20	21	22	23
24	25	26	27	28	29	30

Each night, what you can see of the moon changes a little bit. After about 7 nights, the moon looks like this:

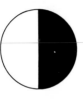

This is called a **half moon**.

Sunday	Monday	Tuesday	Wednesday	Thursday	Friday	Saturday
					1	2
3	4	 5	6	7	8	9
10	11	12	13	14	15	16
17	18	19	20	21	22	23
24	25	26	27	28	29	30

What you can see of the moon keeps changing, night after night. After about 7 more nights, you can't see the moon at all. This is called a **new moon**.

Sunday	Monday	Tuesday	Wednesday	Thursday	Friday	Saturday
					1	2
3	4	5	6	7	8	9
10	11	12	13	14	15	16
17	18	19	20	21	22	23
24	25	26	27	28	29	30

Then, night after night, you can see
more and more of the moon in the light.
After about 7 more nights, you can see a
half moon again.

Sunday	Monday	Tuesday	Wednesday	Thursday	Friday	Saturday
					1	2
3	4	5	6	7	8	9
10	11	12	13	14	15	16
17	18	19	20	21	22	23
24	25	26	27	28	29	30

After about 7 more nights, you see a full moon again.

Each month, the moon goes from full moon to half moon to new moon to half moon to full moon.

Look at the night sky. Can you see the moon? How does the moon look tonight?

Sharing the Joy of Reading

Beginning readers enjoy reading books on their own. Reading a book is a worthwhile activity in and of itself for a young reader. However, a child's reading can be even more rewarding if it is shared. This sharing can enhance your child's appreciation — both of the book and of his or her own abilities.

Now that your child has read **Does the Moon Change Shape?**, you can help extend your child's reading experience by encouraging him or her to:

- Retell the story or key concepts presented in this story in his or her own words. The retelling can be oral or written.

- Create a picture of a favorite character, event, or concept from this book.

- Express his or her own ideas and feelings about the subject of this book and other things he or she might want to know about this subject.

Here is an activity that you can do together to help extend your child's appreciation of this book: You and your child can learn more about the moon. Each day the moon rises at a different time. You and your child can observe and record your citings of the moon. (Note: Most newspapers include information about the phases of the moon on the weather page.) After a week, review the changes you have observed in the moon, and see if you can find a pattern. Also, you might want to visit a local planetarium, science museum, or local library to learn more about the moon and the night sky.